INSIDE MLB

TEXAS

RANGERS

BY PATRICK DONNELLY

SportsZone

An Imprint of Abdo Publishing

abdobooks.com

abdobooks.com

Published by Abdo Publishing, a division of ABDO, PO Box 398166, Minneapolis, Minnesota 55439.

Printed in the United States of America, North Mankato, Minnesota.
102022
012023

THIS BOOK CONTAINS RECYCLED MATERIALS

Cover Photo: Joe Robbins/Icon Sportswire/AP Images
Interior Photos: Rick Yeatts/Getty Images Sport/Getty Images, 4; Focus on Sport/Getty Images Sport/Getty Images, 7, 12; Ron Vesely/MLB Images/Getty Images Sport/Getty Images, 9; MLB Photos/Hulton Archive/Getty Images, 10; Bill Janscha/AP Images, 15; Eric Gay/AP Images, 17; Larry Goren/Four Seam Images/AP Images, 18; John Todd/AP Images, 21; Linda Kaye/AP Images, 22; David J. Phillip/AP Images, 25; Mike Carlson/AP Images, 27; Tony Gutierrez/AP Images, 28; Paul Sancya/AP Images, 31; Charlie Riedel/AP Images, 32; Brad Mangin/Major League Baseball/Getty Images, 35; Dilip Vishwanat/Getty Images Sport/Getty Images, 36; LM Otero/AP Images, 37; Tom Szczerbowski/Getty Images Sport/Getty Images, 39; Darren Yamashita/AP Images, 41

Editor: Charlie Beattie
Series Designer: Becky Daum

Library of Congress Control Number: 2022940494

Publisher's Cataloging-in-Publication Data

Names: Donnelly, Patrick, author.
Title: Texas Rangers / by Patrick Donnelly
Description: Minneapolis, Minnesota: Abdo Publishing, 2023 | Series: Inside MLB | Includes online resources and index.
Identifiers: ISBN 9781098290351 (lib. bdg.) | ISBN 9781098275556 (ebook)
Subjects: LCSH: Texas Rangers (Baseball team)--Juvenile literature. | Baseball teams--Juvenile literature. | Professional sports--Juvenile literature. | Sports franchises--Juvenile literature. | Major League Baseball (Organization)--Juvenile literature.
Classification: DDC 796.35764--dc23

TABLE OF CONTENTS

CHAPTER 1

FROM DC TO DALLAS

As he had done so many times before, Adrián Beltré rocked back and forth in the right-handed batters' box. His Texas Rangers were down 4–0 to the Baltimore Orioles in the bottom of the fourth inning on July 30, 2017. But the fans at Globe Life Park in Arlington were still on their feet. They didn't care about the score. They were excited only about the possibility of witnessing history.

The 38-year-old Beltré had been one of the Rangers' most popular players since joining the team in 2011. Over the course of his long career with four teams, he had been a consistent hitter and a terrific fielder at third base. He had also won over fans with his enjoyable personality. He was often seen joking

Adrián Beltré, *left*, hugs his son Adrián Jr. after collecting his 3,000th major league hit on July 30, 2017.

and laughing with teammates and opponents in the middle of tense games. Everyone in Major League Baseball (MLB) was rooting for the likeable star in this at-bat.

Orioles lefty Wade Miley delivered a 3–0 pitch, and Beltré smacked it just inside the third-base line. The crowd erupted as the ball reached the outfield and bounced off the wall. Beltré jogged into second for a double.

The game stopped. Every other Rangers player ran to the top step of the dugout and began clapping before surrounding their teammate on the field. Beltré's three children rushed out of the stands to greet him. After that, his two daughters and one son went to right field. There they unveiled a banner that read: "Adrián Beltré: 3,000 career hits."

One of baseball's most enjoyable stars had just joined one of the sport's most exclusive clubs. And the 31st player ever to reach 3,000 career hits had done it wearing a Rangers uniform.

HISTORIC HIT

The Caribbean nation of the Dominican Republic has been turning out MLB stars since the 1950s. But Adrián Beltré was the first player from his home country ever to reach 3,000 hits. Less than a year later, Albert Pujols became the second when he collected hit number 3,000 on May 4, 2018.

POWER MOVE

Beltré followed a long line of sluggers who have played for the Rangers franchise. But in the

Towering slugger Frank Howard led the AL in home runs in 1968 and again in 1970.

beginning, those homers didn't fly into the Texas night. The Rangers began as the Senators in Washington, DC, in 1961. The expansion team was a replacement for an older version of the Washington Senators. The first team with that name had just moved to Minnesota and become the Twins.

The replacement Senators were built through an expansion draft. Because other teams can protect certain players from being selected, stars weren't available. As a result, the Senators weren't very good. They lost 100 or more games in each of their first four seasons. From 1961 to 1968, their best finish was sixth place in the 10-team American League (AL).

The Senators' best player was slugging outfielder Frank Howard. He checked in at 6 feet, 7 inches and 255 pounds. That earned him the nickname "the Washington Monument." Howard arrived in a trade with the Los Angeles Dodgers after the 1964 season. He soon became one of the AL's most feared power threats. From 1967 to 1970, Howard led MLB with 172 home runs.

In 1969 the Senators hired Hall of Famer Ted Williams as their manager. Williams was one of the league's best-ever hitters. In Washington he had an instant impact. That year the Senators won 86 games. They also drew more than 900,000 fans for the first time.

The success didn't last. And the crowds soon shrank. Owner Bob Short was losing money and wanted to sell the team. When he didn't get an offer he liked, Short decided to move the Senators. Late in the 1971 season, Short announced that the team would be moving to the Dallas–Fort Worth area. The decision angered Senators fans. They showed they had finally had enough during the team's final home game in Washington. With two outs in the top of the ninth, fans stormed the field and refused to leave. The umpires declared a forfeit in favor of the visiting New York Yankees. When the game was called, Washington was leading 7–5. It was an ugly end to the Senators' time in Washington.

Ted Williams managed the team for its final three seasons in Washington and its first year in Texas.

GO WEST

The move to the Dallas suburb of Arlington didn't work out as Short had hoped. The Rangers failed to draw 700,000 fans in either of their first two years. The hot, muggy weather was one problem. But the team's poor play didn't help. The Rangers lost 100 games in 1972, and Williams resigned. His replacement, future Hall of Famer Whitey Herzog, was a rookie manager with a shaky roster. Short fired him in early September. The Rangers went on to lose 105 games that year.

Jeff Burroughs was one of the Rangers' few stars during the team's early seasons in Texas.

Short sold the Rangers early in the 1974 season. One of his final decisions might have been his best. He hired Billy Martin to replace Herzog. The former Yankees infielder had led the Minnesota Twins and Detroit Tigers to division titles within the previous five years. But Martin also wore out his welcome in both spots as he argued with owners, players, and even fans.

His time in Texas followed a similar pattern. In his first full season with the Rangers, Martin led the team to 84 wins and a second-place finish in the AL West. Pitcher Ferguson Jenkins won 25 games. Jeff Burroughs, a 23-year-old right fielder, hit .301 and led the AL with 118 runs batted in (RBIs) to win the AL Most Valuable Player (MVP) Award. But midway through the 1975 season, the team was just 44–51, and Martin was fighting with new owner Brad Corbett. Suddenly, Martin was gone.

Texas's performance picked up later in the decade. The Rangers won 94 games in 1977. Future Hall of Fame pitchers Gaylord Perry and Bert Blyleven combined for 29 wins. That season marked the first of the team's two straight second-place finishes. But it didn't last. The Rangers were soon struggling. It would take another decade for the team to become relevant again.

RUSHED TO THE MAJORS

One of the team's first draft picks in Texas was left-handed pitcher David Clyde. The youngster was considered a phenom, and owner Bob Short wanted him to pitch in the majors right away. The owner thought the young pitcher would help sell tickets. Clyde debuted with the team to a sellout crowd just 20 days after his high school graduation. But the novelty wore off fast. Clyde struggled for the rest of the season. By 1975 Clyde was playing in the minors. Despite coming back up three years later, he was out of the majors by 1980.

T
TEXAS

CHAPTER 2

PLAYOFF PUSH

After a 9–23 start to the 1985 season, the Rangers went looking for a new manager. They found one coaching third base for the New York Mets. Bobby Valentine was only 35 when the Rangers hired him. That made him the youngest manager in the league. He was also possibly the most talkative. Valentine was often found smiling and laughing. His energy helped turn the Rangers around quickly.

Though the team finished 62–99 in his first season, the Rangers bounced back in 1986. There were some talented players on the roster. Knuckleballer Charlie Hough averaged 14 wins per season in the 1980s. Designated hitter Larry Parrish and outfielder Pete Incaviglia were power threats.

Charlie Hough holds several Rangers team pitching records, including career wins, strikeouts, and complete games.

Center fielder Oddibe McDowell was one of the more exciting young players in baseball.

Behind that core, the Rangers finished 87–75 in 1986. It still wasn't good enough to win the AL West. But the second-place finish raised the team's hopes of taking a division title. Instead, the Rangers fell flat the next two seasons, dropping to 70–91 in 1988. By now it was clear Valentine needed some help.

PRESIDENTIAL PRESENCE

In 1989 a group of investors pooled their money to purchase the Rangers from Eddie Chiles. The lead investor was George W. Bush. The son of US president George H. W. Bush served as the managing partner and led the push to acquire funding for a new ballpark. Bush stepped down from daily operations in 1994 when he was elected governor of Texas. He left the Rangers when the team was sold in 1998, two years before following his father's footsteps to the White House.

THE RYAN EXPRESS

McDowell was traded to Cleveland along with two other players for Julio Franco. The infielder thrived in Texas. By 1991 he was the best hitter in the majors, with a .341 average.

However, the key addition was right-hander Nolan Ryan. The Refugio, Texas, native had already played 22 MLB seasons when he joined the Rangers in the winter of 1988. Using his famous "Ryan Express" fastball, he had also led the league in strikeouts nine times and had

Teammates carry Nolan Ryan off the field after his no-hitter against the Toronto Blue Jays on May 1, 1991.

thrown five no-hitters. Even though he was 41, Ryan showed he had plenty of gas left.

Over the next five years, Ryan reached several milestones. In August 1989, he became the first pitcher in league history to reach 5,000 career strikeouts. A year later, he threw his sixth no-hitter. He struck out 14 Oakland Athletics in a 5–0 win. Seven weeks after that, he won his 300th game.

On May 1, 1991, Ryan caused jaws to drop throughout the league again with his seventh career no-hitter. He fanned 16 Toronto Blue Jays in a 3–0 win. His final out came on a strikeout of future Hall of Famer Roberto Alomar. At age 44, Ryan became the oldest pitcher to throw a no-hitter in MLB history.

Rangers fans packed the stadium whenever Ryan pitched. And he helped the Rangers win consistently. Between 1989 and 1991, Ryan and Valentine helped Texas achieve three straight winning seasons.

However, even that wasn't enough to get Texas to the playoffs, which included only two teams per league at the time. And when the Rangers started slowly in 1992, Valentine was replaced by former Rangers star Toby Harrah on the bench. After the season, Kevin Kennedy took over the job.

PLAYOFFS AT LAST

The Rangers won 86 games and finished in second place in Kennedy's first year. Ryan retired after the season, at age 46. But even without him, the Rangers were on pace to set a team attendance record in 1994. A big reason for this was the ballpark itself. After 22 seasons in Arlington Stadium, the Rangers had a new home. The Ballpark in Arlington opened and soon saw a highlight. Lefty Kenny Rogers threw the team's first-ever perfect game on July 28.

Just 15 days after Rogers's masterpiece, things went south for the entire league. A players' strike ended the season. The postseason and World Series were eventually canceled.

Kenny Rogers, *left*, is greeted by first baseman Will Clark, *right*, and catcher Iván Rodríguez after the final out of Rogers's perfect game in 1994.

The Rangers had been set up to reach the playoffs, which were expanded that year to four teams per league. The Rangers were in first place when the season shut down. However, they still weren't a great team. The AL West was a weak division in 1994. The Rangers were leading it with a record of just 52–62. Kennedy was let go before the 1995 season and replaced by Johnny Oates.

Juan González topped 40 home runs five times in the 1990s while playing for the Rangers.

After a winning season in 1995, the Rangers finally broke through a year later. The 1996 team had five starting pitchers win at least 11 games. Righties Bobby Witt and Ken Hill each won 16. That was enough to back up a solid offense. Third baseman Dean Palmer and left fielder Rusty Greer each drove in 100 runs. Catcher Iván "Pudge" Rodríguez had a breakout offensive season. He hit .300 and scored 116 runs. The 24-year-old also added his fifth straight Gold Glove Award for excellent defense.

The Rangers' main power threat was right fielder Juan González. He won AL MVP after hitting .314 with 47 homers and 144 RBIs. And with a 90–72 record, Texas was finally a playoff team after a 25-year wait.

While the journey was long to reach the postseason, the Rangers' first playoff win came quickly. Texas knocked off the New York Yankees 6–2 in Game 1 of the AL Division Series (ALDS). González and Palmer led the way. Each homered in a five-run fourth inning.

Texas had a 4–1 lead early in Game 2 at Yankee Stadium. But a chance to head home one win away from series victory slipped away. New York eventually tied the game 4–4 in the eighth inning and won it in the 12th.

Back in Texas, more than 50,000 fans packed the stands to watch the Rangers' first home playoff game.

Unfortunately, they saw another heartbreaker. The Yankees scored twice in the ninth to steal a 3–2 win in Game 3. New York finished off the series the next day, breaking a 4–4 tie in the seventh inning on its way to a 6–4 win.

SWINGS AND MISSES

The closer for the Yankees in Games 3 and 4 was righty John Wetteland. After the season, Texas signed him away from New York. Wetteland helped Texas get back to the playoffs in 1998. That year he saved 42 games. Meanwhile, González won another MVP Award. In an incredible season, he hit .318 with 45 homers and 157 RBIs. He also smacked 50 doubles. But the Rangers ran into the Yankees again in the playoffs. A 3–0 ALDS loss sent Texas home early. González hit just 1-for-12 against New York pitching. The Rangers scored only one run in the series.

In 1999 it was Rodríguez's turn to claim MVP honors. He hit .332 with 35 homers and 113 RBIs. The Ballpark in Arlington was proving to be a hitter's paradise. González, Greer, and first baseman/designated hitter Rafael Palmeiro also racked up big numbers. The Rangers won a team-record 95 games.

However, the 1999 playoffs were nearly an exact copy of 1998. The Rangers faced the Yankees again. New York was on its way to a third World Series win in four years. And again, the

Iván Rodríguez won 10 consecutive Gold Glove Awards as the top fielding catcher in the AL from 1992 to 2001.

Yankees shut down the Rangers' bats. Texas scored just a single run for a second straight year while losing 3–0.

It was a tough end to the best seasons in Rangers history. The team responded by trading González to the Detroit Tigers. And when they fell to last place in 2000, the Rangers responded by making the biggest free-agent splash in MLB history.

RANG
3

BIG MONEY

By the end of the 2000 season, many thought shortstop Alex Rodriguez could end up as one of the greatest players in baseball history. And he was still only 24. Rodriguez had topped 40 homers each of the previous three seasons. As a 20-year-old in 1996, he led the league with a .358 average. And "A-Rod" was now a free agent.

The Rangers blew away the competition when it came to signing the young star. The contract the team offered was twice as big as any contract handed out in any American sport. To bring Rodriguez to Texas, owner Tom Hicks shelled out $252 million over 10 seasons.

Alex Rodriguez led the AL in home runs during each of his three seasons in Texas.

"Alex is the player we believe will allow this franchise to fulfill its dream of continuing on its path to becoming a World Series champion," Hicks said.

It didn't quite work out that way. The shortstop put up incredible stats. In the first three years of his deal, Rodriguez averaged 52 home runs and 132 RBIs. He also won two Gold Gloves and was the AL MVP in 2003. But in all three years, the Rangers finished last in the AL West.

BEHIND THE NUMBERS

The contract Alex Rodriguez signed with the Rangers in 2000 was mind-boggling on many levels. His $25.2 million annual salary was more than the Minnesota Twins, Kansas City Royals, and Milwaukee Brewers paid their entire teams in 2000. The $252 million total was $2 million more than Tom Hicks had paid for the Rangers, the ballpark, and 270 acres of land surrounding the park in 1998. By 2022, several MLB players had signed larger contracts. One of them was Rodriguez himself, who signed a $275 million deal with the New York Yankees in 2008.

Rodriguez's only problem was that he didn't pitch. In 2001 the Rangers had a team earned-run average (ERA) of 5.71, the worst in baseball. Two years later, it was 5.67, again at the bottom of the league. The team's farm system wasn't developing young pitchers. And a host of free-agent signings didn't work out.

Eventually the Rangers decided to end the A-Rod experiment. After the 2003 season, they traded him to

Sluggers like Michael Young, *left*, Alfonso Soriano, *center*, and Hank Blalock, *right*, helped the Rangers maintain a powerful offense during the 2000s.

the New York Yankees for second baseman Alfonso Soriano. Despite losing one of the game's biggest stars, the Rangers improved. Led by All-Star play from Soriano and new shortstop Michael Young, the Rangers won 89 games in 2004. But it was still only good enough for third place in a tough division.

MOVING ON

Young won the AL batting title in 2005 as he continued to blossom. But the team struggled to replace the power of the departed Rodriguez.

The Rangers' next slugger finally arrived in 2008, though it took him a lot longer to get to the majors than expected. Josh Hamilton was the prize of the 1999 MLB Draft. The Tampa Bay Devil Rays selected the talented high school outfielder with the first overall pick. He was viewed as a true five-tool player, one who could hit for power and average, run, throw, and play strong defense.

However, Hamilton's career was soon derailed by injuries and drug addiction. He was out of baseball entirely for three years as he fought to recover from his substance abuse. In 2007 the Cincinnati Reds took a chance on Hamilton, and he did well as a part-time player.

The Rangers had seen enough. They traded two young pitchers to Cincinnati for Hamilton and made him their everyday center fielder in 2008. He responded with a massive year, leading the AL with 130 RBIs and earning an All-Star spot. The Rangers began to build around Hamilton, eventually

STEROID SLUGGERS

Steroids were a huge problem in baseball throughout the late 1980s and 1990s. After the league started cracking down in the early 2000s, many of the game's greatest stars were caught using performance-enhancing drugs (PEDs). That included Alex Rodriguez and Rafael Palmeiro. Many other Rangers stars were suspected of using PEDs in the 1990s, when the team was one of the most powerful home run–hitting clubs in the major leagues.

Josh Hamilton led the majors with a .359 batting average in 2010.

putting together a lineup that rivaled their heavy-hitting playoff teams of the late 1990s.

BREAKING THROUGH

By 2010 the Rangers were winners again. The team had won 87 games the year before, featuring a power lineup that included

C. J. Wilson delivers a pitch during Game 1 of the 2010 ALCS against the New York Yankees.

Hamilton, Young, right fielder Nelson Cruz, second baseman Ian Kinsler, and shortstop Elvis Andrus. But they added even more firepower by bringing in former MVP Vladimir Guerrero.

One of the best hitters of his generation, the 35-year-old drove in a team-high 115 runs.

Manager Ron Washington's team still needed a pitching ace. The Rangers found one in their own bullpen. Lefty C. J. Wilson had been a reliever for the previous four seasons. In 2010 he became a starter. At one point, he won seven straight decisions while finishing 15–8. The late-season addition of veteran lefty Cliff Lee also helped the staff. Young closer Neftalí Feliz locked down games in the ninth inning. The 22-year-old righty saved 40 games with an overpowering fastball.

The Rangers took over first place for good in early June and never looked back. Their 90–72 record won the AL West by nine games. That set up a matchup with Tampa Bay in the ALDS. Lee won the opener, and then Wilson and two relievers combined for a 6–0 shutout in Game 2.

One win away from the team's first playoff series victory, the Rangers stumbled and lost two straight. Lee took the hill again in Game 5. In a dominant performance, the lefty struck out 11 and allowed only one run. The Rangers won 5–1.

THE FALL CLASSIC

The team didn't spend much time celebrating the milestone. Texas had to face the defending World Series champion Yankees in the AL Championship Series (ALCS). And after New

York scored five runs in the eighth inning of Game 1 to win 6–5, it looked like a repeat of the teams' 1990s matchups.

However, this was a different Rangers team. They outscored the Yankees 25–5 while winning the next three games. After a 7–2 stumble in Game 5 at Yankee Stadium, the Rangers headed home with two more chances.

A crowd of 51,000 fans turned out at the Ballpark in Arlington for Game 6. They hoped to see team history. It was still 1–1 in the fifth when Guerrero smacked a two-run double. The Rangers scored four times in the inning. On the mound, righty Colby Lewis was having the game of his career. He held the Yankees to only three hits over eight innings as Texas won 6–1. Three decades after arriving in Texas, the Rangers were finally headed to the World Series.

Waiting for the Rangers were the San Francisco Giants. The Giants had not won a World Series since 1954, when the team still played in New York. And it was San Francisco's drought that ended. The Giants roughed up Lee in an 11–7 Game 1 win.

Texas was in a 2–0 hole when Lewis delivered another strong start in Game 3. But the 4–2 victory was as good as things got for Texas. The Giants held the Rangers to just one run over the next two games to claim the title. It was a tough ending for the Rangers, but more thrills were right around the corner.

The Rangers pile on each other to celebrate reaching the franchise's first World Series berth after beating the Yankees in Game 6 of the 2010 ALCS.

TEXAS

CHAPTER 4

OH, SO CLOSE

The Rangers bounced back from their 2010 disappointment by putting together the best season in team history. The team still had stars in Josh Hamilton, Nelson Cruz, Ian Kinsler, Elvis Andrus, and Michael Young. Vladimir Guerrero left but was replaced in the lineup by new power-hitting third baseman Adrián Beltré. Pitchers C. J. Wilson and Colby Lewis returned. Young starters Derek Holland, Matt Harrison, and flame-throwing Alexi Ogando joined them. All five starters won at least 13 games.

The Rangers won a franchise-best 96 games. In the playoffs, they overcame the Tampa Bay Rays in the ALDS. Cruz then starred against the Detroit Tigers in the ALCS. He hit six home

Nelson Cruz celebrates on his way to first base after his grand slam in Game 2 of the 2011 ALCS.

runs, including a walk-off grand slam in Game 2. The offensive explosion paced the Rangers to a 4–2 series victory.

The National League champion St. Louis Cardinals were waiting in the World Series. Pitching dominated early. Cardinals ace Chris Carpenter outdueled Wilson in a 3–2 St. Louis win in Game 1. Lewis was excellent in Game 2, but Texas trailed 1–0 heading into the top of the ninth. The Rangers scored twice before Feliz shut the door in the bottom half to even things up.

AN EPIC BATTLE

The Cardinals exploded for a 16–7 Game 3 victory. But Rangers pitching bounced back. Over the next two games in Texas, Holland and Wilson delivered strong starts. The Rangers won 4–0 and 4–2. Suddenly they were just one win away from a championship.

Game 6 in St. Louis turned out to be one of the most dramatic games in World Series history. Texas built three separate one-run leads early in the game. But the Cardinals fought back each time. In the seventh inning, the Rangers opened a 7–4 lead on back-to-back homers from Beltré and Cruz and a Kinsler RBI single.

With two outs and two on in the ninth and the score 7–5, Cardinals third baseman David Freese batted against Feliz. The Rangers' reliever worked a 3–2 count, but Freese belted

Derek Holland allowed only two hits in 8 1/3 innings during Game 4 of the 2011 World Series.

the payoff pitch to right field. Cruz couldn't track it down, and it went for a triple. Both runners scored to send the game to extra innings.

In the 10th, Hamilton smacked a two-run homer to put Texas up 9–7. Once again, the Rangers were three outs away. But St. Louis scraped back two runs in the bottom half off two Texas relievers. Once again, the game-tying hit came with two

Adrián Beltré, *second from right*, is congratulated by teammates after hitting a home run in Game 6 of the 2011 World Series.

outs and two strikes on St. Louis's Lance Berkman. The amazing game went on.

It finally ended in the bottom of the 11th. Freese homered to center off Texas's Mark Lowe to win it 10–9. The Rangers had been one strike away from a championship twice only to lose.

RBI doubles from Hamilton and Young got Game 7 off to a good start. However, it was all St. Louis from there. The Cardinals tied the game in the bottom of the first on another big hit by Freese. They took the lead in the third. Texas couldn't find any more offensive answers against Carpenter and four St. Louis relievers. A 6–2 defeat was a bitter pill for Texas fans after the drama of Game 6.

The Rangers paid $51.7 million to the Hokkaido Nippon Ham Fighters in Japan for the rights to sign pitcher Yu Darvish in December 2011.

ARRIVALS AND DEPARTURES

The Rangers put the World Series disappointment behind them to win 93 games in 2012. But that was only good enough for an appearance in the AL wild-card game. Texas lost 5–1 to the Baltimore Orioles.

The starter for Texas in that game was right-hander Yu Darvish. The 26-year-old was in his first MLB season after several years as a superstar in his native Japan. He continued his strong play in Texas, leading the league in strikeouts during the 2013 season.

While players like Darvish came in, several veteran Rangers left. Hamilton hit 43 homers in 2012, but he signed with the division-rival Los Angeles Angels after the season. Longtime fan favorite Young had debuted with the Rangers in 2000. He left before the 2013 season as the franchise's all-time leader in games played.

In 2013 the Rangers won their final seven regular-season games to force a one-game playoff with the Rays for the AL wild-card spot. Texas's big bats couldn't handle Tampa Bay lefty David Price in a 5–2 loss. After the season, Cruz left as a free agent, and Kinsler was traded away.

TORONTO DRAMA

Injuries to the pitching staff destroyed the 2014 season, but the Rangers were back in the playoffs in 2015. Their ALDS opponents were the Toronto Blue Jays. After Texas won the first two games, Toronto battled back to tie the series. That set up a drama-filled Game 5 in Toronto.

The game was tied 2–2 in the top of the seventh when a bizarre play gave Texas the lead. Right fielder Shin-Soo Choo was at the plate, with runner Rougned Odor on third and two out. After a pitch, the throw from Toronto catcher Russell Martin hit Choo's bat by mistake. The ball rolled away, and Odor sprinted home. Umpire Dale Scott signaled that the ball

Rougned Odor, *right*, celebrates with Prince Fielder, *left*, after Odor scored the controversial go-ahead run in Game 5 of the 2015 ALDS.

was dead and ordered Odor back to third. After an umpires' conference, the call was changed, and the run counted.

The fans at Toronto's Rogers Center erupted. They started pelting the field with whatever they could find to throw. The game was delayed for 18 minutes before order could be restored.

The Rangers didn't score again in the inning. Toronto came up in the bottom half frustrated and took it out on the Texas pitching staff. After a fielder's choice tied the game, Blue Jays slugger José Bautista launched a long three-run homer to left. As he watched it, Bautista flipped his bat high in the air. The Rangers felt this was poor sportsmanship. Tempers flared, and players came onto the field to confront each other before the next at-bat. Things finally calmed down, but the emotional, 54-minute inning finished off the Rangers. The 6–3 score held, and Texas was eliminated.

The two teams met again in the ALDS the next season. Despite two close games, the series was far less wild. Toronto knocked out the Rangers in a three-game sweep.

A NEW HOME

Fans still had a chance to root on Beltré's quest for 3,000 hits even though the Rangers had dropped below .500 in 2017. The popular third baseman eventually retired after the 2018 season as the all-time hit leader among players born outside the United States.

Soon the Rangers had something new to look forward to. After nearly three decades at Globe Life Park, formerly the Ballpark in Arlington, the Rangers had a new stadium. Globe Life Field opened in 2020. The new park included a retractable roof to keep it protected from Texas's summer heat.

WORLD SERIES HOSTS

Globe Life Field in Arlington hosted the World Series the year the stadium opened, though the Rangers didn't get to play in it. The 2020 MLB season was shortened due to the COVID-19 pandemic. The league decided to hold its playoffs at neutral sites to limit travel. The entire 2020 World Series was held at Globe Life Field, with the Los Angeles Dodgers beating the Tampa Bay Rays in six games for the title.

Shortstop Corey Seager signed the most expensive contract in Rangers history when he joined the team on December 1, 2021.

Before the 2022 season, the Rangers spent big money to fill their stadium with new stars. The team signed former Los Angeles Dodgers shortstop Corey Seager to a $325 million contract. The Rangers also signed second baseman Marcus Semien to a deal worth $175 million. Texas fans hoped it was the start of a rebuild that would finally take them to the top.

TIMELINE

1961

The Washington Senators debut as one of two American League expansion teams.

1972

After 11 mostly dismal seasons in Washington, the team moves to the Dallas–Fort Worth area and is renamed the Texas Rangers.

1974

Right fielder Jeff Burroughs wins the AL MVP Award.

1978

The Rangers trade All-Star shortstop Toby Harrah to Cleveland for fellow All-Star infielder Buddy Bell.

1985

Bobby Valentine is hired as manager.

1988

Nolan Ryan signs with the Rangers as a free agent.

1990

Seven weeks after pitching his sixth career no-hitter, Ryan beats the Brewers for his 300th career victory.

1991

Ryan throws his seventh and final no-hitter against the Toronto Blue Jays.

1996

The Rangers win their first division title and make their first playoff appearance, losing to the New York Yankees in the ALDS.

1999

Texas wins its third straight AL West title and loses to the Yankees in the ALDS for the third time in four years.

2000

Shortstop Alex Rodriguez signs a record-setting 10-year, $252 million contract with the Rangers.

2010

The Rangers reach the World Series for the first time but lose to the Giants in five games.

2011

In an epic seven-game battle, the St. Louis Cardinals come back to beat the Rangers in the final two games to win the World Series.

2015

The Rangers win the first of two straight AL West titles but fall to the Blue Jays in the ALDS both years.

2017

Adrián Beltré collects his 3,000th career hit.

2020

Globe Life Field opens in Arlington and hosts the World Series between the Dodgers and Rays.

2021

After finishing 60–102, the Rangers commit $500 million in contracts to free-agent infielders Corey Seagar and Marcus Semien in December.

TEAM FACTS

FRANCHISE HISTORY

Washington Senators (1961–71)
Texas Rangers (1972–)

KEY PLAYERS

Elvis Andrus (2009–20)
Buddy Bell (1979–85, 1989)
Adrián Beltré (2011–18)
Jeff Burroughs (1970–76)
Juan González (1989–99, 2002–03)
Rusty Greer (1994–2002)
Josh Hamilton (2008–12, 2015)
Toby Harrah (1969, 1971–78, 1985–86)
Charlie Hough (1980–90)
Frank Howard (1965–72)
Rafael Palmeiro (1989–93, 1999–2003)
Alex Rodriguez (2001–03)
Iván Rodríguez (1991–2002, 2009)
Kenny Rogers (1989–95, 2000–02, 2004–05)
Nolan Ryan (1989–93)
Jim Sundberg (1974–83, 1988–89)
Michael Young (2000–12)

KEY MANAGERS

Johnny Oates (1995–2001)
Bobby Valentine (1985–92)
Ron Washington (2007–14)

HOME STADIUMS

Griffith Stadium (1961)
RFK Stadium (1962–71)
Arlington Stadium (1972–93)
Globe Life Park in Arlington (1994–2019)
Also known as:
The Ballpark in Arlington (1994–2004)
Ameriquest Field (2004–07)
Rangers Ballpark in Arlington (2007–13)
Globe Life Field (2020–)

TEAM TRIVIA

GO TO BED!

On June 12, 1967, the Senators and White Sox played a 22-inning game that ended at 2:43 a.m. local time. After that, MLB adopted a rule that said no inning can start after 1 a.m. If the game is still going at that point, it is paused and finished the next day.

HOT STREAK

Rangers outfielder Kevin Mench went on a tear in April 2006. He blasted a home run in eight straight games. That's one shy of the MLB record, but it's the longest streak for a right-handed hitter.

CIRCLE THE BASES

On August 27, 1977, the Rangers accomplished a rare feat. Toby Harrah and Bump Wills hit inside-the-park home runs on consecutive pitches from the Yankees' Ken Clay in New York.

DERBY DINGERS

Josh Hamilton put on a record-setting display at the 2008 Home Run Derby at Yankee Stadium. In the first round, Hamilton hit 28 home runs on 38 swings. At one point, he homered on 13 straight pitches. Three of his homers traveled more than 500 feet.

GLOSSARY

ace

A team's best starting pitcher.

bullpen

The area of a baseball field where relief pitchers warm up; also used to refer to a team's relievers as a group.

closer

A pitcher who comes in at the end of the game to secure a win for his team.

fielder's choice

A batted ball with runners on base on which a batter reaches a base safely because a fielder attempts to make a play on one of the existing baserunners.

free agent

A player whose rights are not owned by any team.

no-hitter

A complete game in which a team does not allow any hits.

perfect game

A complete game in which a team does not allow any batter to reach base.

players' strike

When players refuse to work due to a disagreement between them and their employers (teams) about things such as working conditions or wages.

postseason

Another word for playoffs; the time after the end of the regular season when teams play to determine a champion.

shutout

A complete game in which a team allows no runs.

veteran

A player who has played for many years.

MORE INFORMATION

BOOKS

Flynn, Brendan. *The MLB Encyclopedia*. Minneapolis, MN: Abdo Publishing, 2022.

Gitlin, Marty. *MLB*. Minneapolis, MN: Abdo Publishing, 2021.

Hewson, Anthony K. *GOATs of Baseball*. Minneapolis, MN: Abdo Publishing, 2022.

ONLINE RESOURCES

Booklinks
NONFICTION NETWORK
FREE! ONLINE NONFICTION RESOURCES

To learn more about the Texas Rangers, please visit **abdobooklinks.com** or scan this QR code. These links are routinely monitored and updated to provide the most current information available.

INDEX

ABOUT THE AUTHOR

Patrick Donnelly is a freelance writer who lives in Minneapolis, Minnesota. He has covered Major League Baseball for more than 20 years.